The Ambassador of the 14th Hole

The Inspiring Story of
Matthew Jarrett Mason

As Told By
Mary Mason and Others

matthew J mason

Published by

IN HIS STEPS PUBLISHING
6500 Clito Road
Statesboro, GA 30461
(912) 587-4400 (DrRev@msn.com)
http://www.ihspub.com

Cover Photo by Dr. Charles E. Cravey

ISBN: 978-1-58535-197-8

Editor's Preface

It was one of those "Get Acquainted" meetings, late in December of 2009 on Hilton Head Island, South Carolina, when I first met "Matt," as he prefers to be called.

My wife, Renee, and I entered the home of Dick and Mary Mason in order for me to glean photos and background info from Matt's mother, Mary, for a proposed book I was planning to publish for her. The book would be about Matt (Matthew), who was born a Down's syndrome baby. Now 40, Matt has lived a most interesting life, and has been known by practically everyone on Hilton Head. Shortly after arriving in their home, Renee and I would discover why Matt was so popular.

With heavy winds and temps in the low forties, Renee and I left our car in the parking area and ascended the staircase to Dick and Mary's front door. Dick opened the door and greeted us, and immediately Matt stepped out around his dad and began to hug Renee and I with fervor! He gently kissed my wife on the cheek and said, "I love you." He clung to us both and seemed so appreciative for our presence there and the fact that I would be publishing this book about his life.

Matt was home for Christmas. He has been living in a group home with three other housemates in Maryland. There, Matt has become very independent. Matt doesn't appear to be forty years of age, instead, he appeared to me to be around eighteen to twenty. His enthusiasm for life is contagious. He is a bundle of joy and excitement, and his demeanor never seems to change. He loves telling jokes and making people laugh, and he instantly stole our hearts that day!

Matt took me to his bedroom where he anxiously showed me photos he and his mom had put together for the book. He hugged me again and called me "Doc!"

We then left the apartment to have lunch at TidePointe with Dick, Mary, Matt and some friends of the family. Around the table, Matt was the center of attention, sharing jokes and exuding that million-dollar smile!

We then took a drive to Harbour Town Golf Club where the annual Heritage Pro Golf Tournament is held, the week following the Master's. There we met with John Farrell—Golf Pro of Harbour Town, and Dr. Dan Hofmann—an avid volunteer for the tournament each year. We weathered blustery, cool weather in golf carts as we made our way to the 18th Green where I took photos for the book. Matt was thoroughly excited and the cool, crisp air did not seem to bother him at all.

John Farrell—Matthew—Dr. Dan Hoffmann

Matt has been dubbed "The Ambassador of the 14th Hole" at the Heritage because he volunteers each year to silence the crowds during the tournament on that particular hole. All of the Pro's know Matt and often take time during the Tournament to walk over and greet him.

Matt's story is a very unique one and is filled with tenderness as well as struggle. Every parent who has raised a Down's syndrome child, will find themselves in Mary Mason's recollections. They are touching and will warm the heart. I am proud to have been brought into Matt's life and look forward to a continuing relationship. I am thankful that Matt's life has now touched mine!

Dr. Charles E. Cravey, Publisher
December 2009

Acknowledgments

Linda Hopkins—spent many hours giving advise and moral support.

Sharon Balmforth—encouraged me (Mary) through her wonderful teaching in the "Writers Anonymous Group".

Jay Marshal—who invited me to the writers group.

Carol Fowler—rescued me from the computer many times!

Dr. Charles Cravey—compiled our work with speed, love and his understanding of our story.

GOD—gave me the courage and audacity to tackle this project.

Dick Mason—allowed me freedom of thought and time. He gave advise when and where it was needed!

CONTENTS

CHAPTER ONE:

Born Special (Mary)

(A success story about a baby born with Down's Syndrome)

Surprise, surprise, "You are pregnant!"

When this news sank into my brain, I adjusted into a rather noble mode. I was forty years old! In my new state of being, I did not wear maternity clothes or eat anything really good for nine months.

My husband, Dick, was happy. I expected him to order cigars with plain bands, not wanting to wait until the baby was born. Those were the days when only God knew the sex of the unborn child.

Our little family gathered around the kitchen table as Dick cleared his throat and announced, "We are going to have another child!" One of our teenagers, Michael, mumbled something like, "You must have been really fooling around!" I do not remember our daughter, Kim, or our seven-year-old son, David, doing anything but staring straight ahead.

Dick and I hastened to explain that this baby was a gift from God. Although unexpected, we would love the baby as much as we had loved Michael, Kim and David. The child would become part of our family and dearly loved by all.

Have you ever received a gift that surprised you beyond all expectations?

Matthew was born with a severe heart defect. The doctors had little choice but to give us a poor prognosis for our new little month-early, four-pound baby boy. We were advised to live day-by-day, expecting him to live only a very short time.

For forty-years now, Matthew's life has touched everyone he meets. He sees the good in each person he encounters. He smiles, he laughs, and he hugs. These are the melodies that blend and harmonize into a love song.

Matt has a zest for life! He seeks the media, microphones, center stage, and being interviewed. Tom Lehman, the internationally known golfer, said of him, "He interviews well."

Matthew never sees a fault in anyone and seldom forgets a face or a name. Reading and writing are a huge part of his life. To please others is his greatest pleasure.

His prayers offered to God are the most sincere ever heard. He has prayed for large gatherings without any advance notice. Most of the time he is joy enveloped in human skin!

This is a story of hope to all who know or have known a special-needs child.

My husband and I are grateful to God for choosing us to parent Matthew. Most of what we need to know about living life, with peace and love, we have learned from Matt.

!

Born Special (Matthew)

Hi, my name is Matthew Jarrett Mason. God decided to send me to a wonderful family. Mary and Dick are my parents, and Michael, Kim and David, are my two brothers and sister.

I was born one month early on August 2, 1969 at the Beebe Hospital in Lewes, Delaware, which was a three day effort on my Mother's part!

My family spend summers at nearby Dewey Beach. When my Mom began to have some signs that her baby (that was me) would be arriving soon, she was told not to travel back to Wilmington, Delaware, where we lived. This is why I was born at the beach.

When I left the Beebe Hospital, my parents took me to our cottage on new Orleans Street in Dewey Beach. It was a very small cottage.

We showered outside, even if it was raining!

When I finally grew hair, it would get orange from the sulfur well water. Every member of my family, except for my dad who had dark brown hair, would have orange hair and toenails by the end of August. We all had blonde hair at the beginning of the summer!

We stayed a week at the beach, then packed everything to go to our home in Wilmington, Delaware.

CHAPTER TWO:

Family (Matthew)

Dick, my Dad, is six-feet-tall. He is a kind man with a pleasant, smiling face. When I was born, he took care of a bunch of things—the yard, the dog, his job with the DuPont Company, and all the activities of my two brothers and sister.

Dad coached, drove to games and practices of sports and gymnastics for all the children.

Mary, my mother, was five-foot-three, an energetic blonde, who took care of everything else our family needed. She was quite the busy lady! Michael and Kim were in High School and David was in third grade when I joined this great and interesting family.

My brothers and sister were getting ready for school and trying to get rid of their orange hair. The orange hair was the result of water from a well at Dewey Beach.

We had a very big house in Wilmington. A living room, dining room, den, kitchen, laundry room, guest bath, four bedrooms, two baths and a sewing room. Guess where my bed was? You guessed it—the sewing room! It seemed large after the small incubator in the Beebe hospital.

!

The Incubator (Matthew)

After I had been home for two weeks, we went to Dr. Hearne, the family pediatrician, for a checkup. He asked my mom to bring me for another visit in two weeks. He said that I had very weak muscles.

During the next visit, Dr. Hearne told my mom to take me to the hospital for my heart was in trouble!

We arrived at the hospital and I was placed in an incubator for my bed in a room they called I.C.U. (Intensive Care Unit).

Heart Failure (Mary)

We were told that Matt was in heart failure! Words cannot begin to describe the fear that pierced my heart.

After our first visit with Dr. Hearne, I had felt a rather foreboding heaviness, something more than sadness, concerning the weak muscles issue. Never did I dream what was to unfold.

For nine days, I would get my family off to school and work and then drive to the hospital to feed little baby, Matt. Taking the precious little one from the incubator, to give the three-ounces of milk, took over an hour.

I was weary physically and mentally with the daily vigils. There were three children and a husband awaiting a report about Matt (and also expecting dinner)!

Gone from my memory are the things our family did to-gether during those first few weeks with our precious new baby. One thing I do clearly remember however, was that we prayed constantly! We somehow arrived at school and work with clean and acceptable attire, properly fed, and with hope-ful smiles on our faces.

We were both concerned and stressed to the max! Why do we seem to forget that God is still in control during these anxious times in our lives?

One morning, after being with Matt in the hospital, WOOPS, would you believe it? I noticed, with great surprise, my car was no longer in the parking space where I had parked each morning.

The space was for early morning parking only, and I had been past the hour's courtesy to move my car. The car had been towed! After a rather large fine, Dick went and re-trieved the car. The next day he went to court to "defend" me. He won! Hearing about a small child in heart failure was enough to convince the judge to return our money.

After a few days in I.C.U., Matt was placed in a ward. Each day, when I arrived to feed Matt, I would hear stories about the nurses and their poor care from other mothers in the ward. I look back on those stressful days wishing I could have done more, listened more, and reacted more, but I was too weary to compute the facts at the time.

One morning, as I entered the hospital ward where Matt's incubator was located, I saw, but could not believe.

"The Climax." Is this possible? The cord to Matt's incubator was on the floor!

I did not know where to turn. When your child is in harm's way, you act with a certain boldness beyond your own strength and think about it later. I quickly put the plug back into the receptacle, fed Matt, and returned home, crying all the way.

I experienced bravery beyond my usual personality. I called the Administrator of the hospital and reported the unbelievable "care" of the nurses (or the lack thereof)! The next day THE RED CARPET was rolled out for me all the way! Hallelujah! God is so good, always watching out for us.

The head nurse was at her most humble and helpful self. I could almost see her at my feet, begging forgiveness for the oversights of the hospital and the poor nursing we had received. The reality was that she was very apologetic. I remember her saying words that would alleviate, hopefully, any ensuing or potential legal actions. This was actually the farthest thing from our minds at that time.

The bottom line was that Matt had a large hole in his heart. Digitalis was prescribed, and after ten days, he came home and life returned to some semblance of normalcy around the Mason household. We were positively not prepared for the changes life was to bring our way.

!

Dewey Beach Photos

Baby Grows (Matthew)

I really did not like milk when I was first born. My mom spent one hour to feed four-ounces into my four pounds. Three years later, I REALLY loved almost every kind of food.

(Mary)

Little did I know that my devotion to Matt's dietary needs would lead him into a world of thinking about food too much. Food seems to have been a problem from the beginning. Matt began life with no interest in food. Now, any food we mention is always his "favorite."

Matt is now an adult, and it is still a challenge to guide him away from too many "favorites." Perhaps this will pass away. We appreciate that he will often exercise. He uses his walking machine most evenings before dinner in his home in Denton, Maryland.

We had a busy household, the activities of two in high school, and a third grader with attention deficit, plus the needs of a premature baby. We all pulled together and managed those challenging first months with our precious new baby.

Dick traveled most every week. He attended the sports and various other activities for three children, and fulfilled the "to do" list of the home, which always included the "doggie" needs and a wonderful vegetable garden. These things often filled his entire weekend at home.

!

Down's Syndrome (Mary)

We were getting adjusted to our life with a new baby, when a call from Dr. Hearne's office informed us that Matt had Down's syndrome.

Blood samples had been sent to a lab in another state, and we were told that the results would take more than several weeks. During this time, I knew in my spirit the results.

I do not recall ever seeing Dick totally break down and cry until that day. I do not recall crying at all.

Remembering those days, even now, is so heart rending. Soon, however, the joy took over. Each day brought new miracles, and we were O.K.!

Forty-years ago there was no internet. There were no informative groups to join. Limited funds allowed only *The Encyclopedia Britannica, Parents Magazine*, and a great deal of common sense.

!

The Swing (Mary)

I rationalized that when muscles were weak, we needed to make them strong by using them. We all began to help Matt move his little legs, and soon he was moving them all by himself.

(Matthew)

The kids went to school and I jumped in my swing. Dr. Hearn had said my muscles were weak. I jumped in my swing that hung on the top of a doorframe.

The whole family helped me learn how to jump, gently bending and pushing my legs. That's why I jumped, and jumped, and jumped! My muscles got strong. Later, when I could walk and then run, I won many blue ribbons for jumping and running with Special Olympics.

(Mary)

When Matt turned three, he attended The Wilmington Special Preschool at the Hanover Presbyterian Church in Wilmington, Delaware.

Each morning at 8:30, Monday through Friday, after our three other children boarded their transportation vehicles, school buses or cars, Matt would climb into the car seat and we would head for preschool. Each of these mornings I would start for school at 8:30 and return at 11:30 in time to pick up Matt from preschool.

Shortly after Matt started preschool, David, our third grader, was enrolled into a private school for children with A.D.D. For two years I added another stop to my morning rounds. This was a routine until, at the age of six, Matt began his "career" at the Bush School, a public school for special needs children. Matt was blessed with a dedicated teacher, Ms. Judy Gallagher.

The Bush School (Matthew)

Bush School taught me so many things. I learned to swim. I joined Boy Scouts. I participated in Special Olympics, and also acted on the stage.

(Mary)

Matt's ability to act was not always exhibited on a stage! His charm was beginning to blossom more each day. How did he know "politically correct" at such an early age?

Another blessing came with Matt's entrance into the Bush School. The school bus would take him to school and return him at 2:30 each day.

David had re-entered public school. Michael and Kim had bus transportation. The happy result was that all my children had a way to get to school!

Matt attended Bush School for six years.

CHARLES W. BUSH SCHOOL
MRS. LINDA MAZEPINK, PRIN.

MRS. GALLAGHER & MRS. POTTS'
CLASS
1981   1982

Matthew is fourth from the left in the middle row!

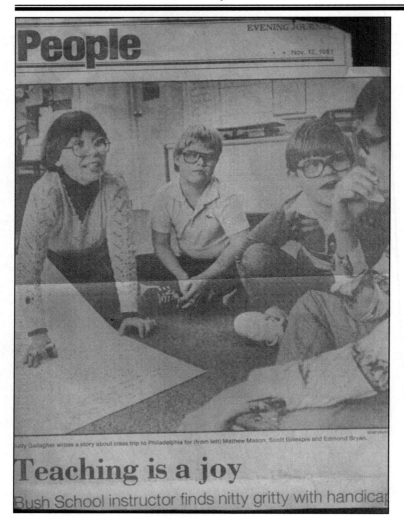

People

EVENING JOURNAL

Nov. 12, 1981

Judy Gallagher writes a story about class trip to Philadelphia for (from left) Mathew Mason, Scott Gillespie and Edmond Bryan.

Teaching is a joy

Bush School instructor finds nitty gritty with handicap

(Caption) "Judy Gallagher writes a story about class trip to Philadelphia for (from left) Matthew Mason, Scott Gillespie and Edmond Bryan.

Tilt (Mary)

As Matt grew, we noticed he always tilted his head to one side. The Bush School recommended that Matt see an ophthalmologist. Matt wore glasses for about two years, but still had the head tilt. One day, while walking in the neighborhood, Dick met Dr. Jennings, a neighbor and eye surgeon. Dick mentioned Matt's problem to him and this resulted in Dr. Jennings welcoming Matt as a new patient.

After our first visit, we learned about Matt's double-vision and how an operation could cure the problem. We look back on Dick's chance meeting with Dr. Jennings and know that was God watching out for us again!

The operation was a success! The double-vision and the head tilt were only a dim memory.

However, a Matt "thing" happened when we visited Dr. Jennings for a final examination. Matt was waiting in the doctor's office alone. When I entered the office, Dr. Jennings looked distressed, telling me that "Matt still tilts his head." I looked over at the little mischievous face and that head straightened very quickly!

Acting is one of Matt's many gifts. I mentioned before that his gifts aren't always demonstrated on a stage!

A.I. DuPont Institute (Matthew)

I was about five when my parents took me to a special group of doctors. The place was called The Alfred I. DuPont Institute, and was located in Wilmington, Delaware.

The doctors said that because I have an extra chromosome, that means I have Down's Syndrome. This was news to me. I think I have never said those two words. I think I ignore the words, Down's Syndrome!

The doctors made appointments for heart tests. Every time we went to a doctor I would have to go to the hospital for another heart test. The nurses would put me on a big, long bed covered with a sheet. I was afraid and tried to get down, then I got the big heavy weights on my chest so I couldn't move. I screamed because I was so afraid. Finally, they took pictures and I got down. I could tell my mom was not so happy either!

Everyone was nice to me and was happy about the things I could do.

My "claim-to-fame" at age six was that I began to learn to read. My mom and Sesame Street taught me how. I could tie my shoes and ride my bike. I was in Special Olympics every year until I went to a school in Maryland. My parents were very happy with me.

Swimming (Matthew)

About my swimming. Sometimes I would get afraid of things that I had not seen or known before. My mother called it, not liking change!

At the Bush School, we had swimming once a week. I did not like the teachers wanting me in the water. I was afraid. One day, since all the teachers were very tired of asking me to get in the water, (I know you guessed it!), Yes, they did push me into the water! I was very surprised, and somehow I scrambled to the edge. The next week Mrs. James pulled me around in the water. Each week I was a little more brave. Soon, I really loved it! I really loved it!

(Mary)

When Matt was very young, he had a few fears: heights, the bathtub, and the swimming pool. The most effective problem-solver was an instructor at the Bush School. A gentle shove and a tenacious boy was soon "dog-paddling."

It was not very long until Matt became a self-taught swimmer. Just a few years later he enjoyed swimming laps. A grown man now, Matt will swim five or more laps in an Olympic sized pool.

My Bike and Where It
Took Me (Matthew)

Riding my bike was something I loved to do. It made me happy and free! At Dewey Beach, when the tide was out, I would ride on the wet sand in big circles and sing.

I would ride to my friend's house in Wilmington, and his mother would call my mother to say I had arrived safely. When it was time to go home, my friend's mother would call my house and then my mom would wait for me to arrive.

One day I did not arrive! I was too young to tell what happened. My parents thought someone had given me a ride in a car because I was delivered to the next neighborhood with my bike (that's what a woman who lived nearby had told us). I didn't know what to do, so I went into the closest house.

"Help! Who are you?" A lady was lying on the couch, trying to recuperate from a migraine headache (we later discovered).

Meanwhile, my mom and dad were looking for me. Finally, they called the police. Seems as if the "Migraine Lady" did the same. I was in some trouble now!

Another time I walked into a house up the street and the lady of the house was there with a gentleman "friend." She was really angry with my parents and me. I always wondered why she was so angry. Was it because her husband was not there?

She could have been the last reason "we" decided I needed a different school.

My parents tried very hard to keep an eye on the many things I would get into.

One day I was playing in a small pool in our backyard when my mom went into the house to answer the telephone. I decided to "check out" the noise at the front of the house. A big truck was pouring black stuff on the driveway next door. I ran across the street to get a better look. I found out that the black stuff was hot. I cried really loud because it was very hot on my bare feet! My mom picked me up and ran as fast as she could to put my HOT black feet in the cool water of our swimming pool. Trust me, that hurt!

All Star Child (Matthew)

I was in a Bush School several years when, at age 10, I was chosen to be the "All Star Child of the Year" for 1980. It was so much fun to be a part of the Wilmington, Delaware, All Star Football Game, played once a year between the North and South high schools.

I played football with the All Star team members, met Miss Delaware, had a bunch of pictures taken, and went to the Governor's office to meet Pete DuPont. That's how he met me! You may have guessed—I was not too excited because we had waited a long time to see him in his office. Trust me!

There were many pictures taken before the big game. There was a picnic, a parade, and practice on the field. I was plain scared and got stubborn when pictures were taken on those open and very high steps at the football field weeks before the big game. I still don't like "see-through" steps! I know now that they are called bleachers.

Another part of the All Star celebration was the big parade in downtown Wilmington. I was able to get the microphone from the man in charge of everything. I sang a little until they took the mike away. Then we marched from the courthouse down the main street in Wilmington. Miss Delaware and I led the parade!

(Mary)

Finally, after all those pictures, parade, meetings and other activities, the day of the big game arrived. About two hours before the game, rain arrived! We parked and scurried quickly to get under the stadium where the band was secure and protected from the weather.

You guessed it—Matt found another mike and was happily singing "New York, New York!" After the third stanza of Matt's rendition, the bandmaster pushed a button on the mike. This permitted no sound from the mike. Matt kept on singing until the rain subsided and the field festivities began.

This was his moment in time. He walked across the field with Miss Delaware and his football "Buddy" while his name and school were announced to a full stadium. Meanwhile, in the bleachers, sat two other Mason's, just beaming.

In 1991, Matt and Alicia Ahearn, an All Star Child from another year, were invited to participate in a fashion show representing the All Star children from several years past.

Matt walked down the runway with Pete Rose, his favorite baseball star, at Longwood Gardens in Pennsylvania.

The Newspaper Route (Matthew)

I did so many things. When I was twelve, I had a job to deliver a weekly newspaper. Friday's after school, mom and I would fold the papers and head out! I had one hundred papers. I think she got more tired than me.

(Mary)

This publication was free. Somehow Matt managed to receive a weekly tip from at least fifty percent of his customers!

Dewey Beach (Matthew)

I spent every summer at Dewey Beach, Delaware, near Lewes, where I was born, before I entered The Benedictine School.

How blessed we were to be in the sun and playing in the sand every day all summer.

Saturday was clean-up day. Some cottages were rented each week and the owner, Granddad Redefer, wanted everything to look neat. All of us picked up trash and put the beach chairs in the right place.

Summer is so wonderful at the beach. I got older and pretty soon able to go with all the gang and their parents to the beach at night. We put our blankets on the sand and sometimes built a fire.

We looked at the stars and tried to name them. We made -up stories about the ocean and the big ships. The ocean waves looked like shiny beads.

The most fun was when we could roast marshmallows and put them on crackers with Hershey chocolate! The kids called them "S'mores."

We did stuff, especially on rainy days. Shells and pieces of wood from the ocean were painted, glued, and changed into wonderful things. Usually, Mrs. Judge would help us. As our neighbor, she took my mom to the hospital to get me born. Her parents, Granddad and Grandmother Redefer, were like family, and we loved them. They owned the land where our cottage was located.

You can guess what we did on sunny days. Off to the beach in the morning, and then home for lunch and a nap. My brothers and sister were with me. Sometimes they read books. We had no television. We always went back to the beach in the afternoons. Everyone swam in the ocean but me! I did not like the loud sound, for it made me afraid.

The Toomey family were our special friends. They lived about four houses from us. Charley, the oldest of the kids, was my first friend. He and his dad would teach me how to fish. All four Toomey children—Kathy, Little Charley, Jennifer and Chris—would always include me as one of the "Gang."

I am an ambassador for God and He started my wonderful journey on this earth right there at Dewey Beach.

(Mary)

Here is an example of a Matthew "Thing":

Scene: The Veterinarian's office in Dewey Beach. It is filled with dogs, cats, and people. Matt has been waiting with Mrs. Toomey for over an hour. He talks to all the animals, looks at a magazine, and finally asks Mrs. Toomey, "How much longer?" He smiles as new animals enter the crowded office, pets her ailing dog, and tries his best to sit still. With all of his ten years of assertiveness, Matt gently stands, blonde "surfer" haircut swinging, and discloses his question to the receptionist: "Don't you know our dog is very, very sick?" They were immediately taken in to see the doctor! This tactic worked well for many different situations, especially in restaurants.

!

A True Friend (Matthew)

I had a special grown-up friend. He and his friends, about twelve of them, would come to the beach every weekend. The girls were GORGEOUS! Everyone was so nice to me. They let me sit with them and play my Christian music. I played my guitar and tapes. However, they would not let me drink their beer! Trust me!

A few years later, my friend got put in prison for selling drugs. Sometimes I would call and pray for him. I would always ask him, "Are your eyes closed?" My mom and dad would take me to see him whenever the prison allowed it. He always sent the small amount of money that he made at his prison job to the Benedictine School. Sister Jeanette also prayed for him. The good news is, he is out of prison, married with two children, and happy. I am tickled!

(Mary)

Never has Matt's friend forgotten those simple, but oh, so sincere prayers! He and his precious family visit often, always remembering the Christmas holidays and birthdays for over twenty-years now.

!

CHAPTER THREE:

ADOLESCENCE

"The Call" (Matthew)

I was spending the summer at the beach. One night I was watching Evangelist Jimmy Swaggart. He is a preacher on T.V. That was the night I really understood what I had known all along—God loved ME and He sent His Son to take my sins. Now I am saved, forever to live with Him in heaven!

So, I decided to get baptized the next time I went to Wilmington. It was pretty funny, because I told my mom, "I want to give my heart to God." The thing is . . . she was driving the car and she was surprised to hear me say those words. After she got the car steadied and straight, we talked about it. Pretty soon, I asked to be baptized. My mom took me to see Pastor Gilbride. He asked me a bunch of questions and then he said, "O.K., you're ready to be baptized."

(Mary)

Dr. Gilbride would often meet with children after church services for a brief chat. On one of these occasions, Matt offered to write Dr. Gilbride's sermons for him, an offer quite promptly refused!

(Matthew)

I thank Gretchen, a friend of my mom's, for taking me and my mom to so many meetings where the truth of God was taught. Gretchen loves the Lord and she helped us to understand how easy it is to be saved, live in heaven forever, and, best of all, have a friend called Jesus who never goes away . . . no matter what!

(Mary)

Matt was baptized in the Brandywine Valley Baptist Church in Wilmington, Delaware. This was Matt's first baptism and profession of faith, but not his last! The First Baptist Church of Jacksonville, Florida, was the next to receive Matt into yet another baptistery.

At this writing, the last time Matt went forward at the end of a church service was December 2009. Dr. Keller said, "Hello, Matt. What are you doing here?"

"I came to tell about the Baby born," Matt replied. Promptly, a five-minute recap of the Christmas story followed and Matt returned to his seat while the congregation smiled, wiped their tears, and applauded.

!

Mild Frenzy (Mary)

As Matt approached the "tween" years, it became clear that different methods to fill the needs of all our children were in order. Matt, an extremely outgoing, inquisitive, and always tenacious young man, needed quite a bit more surveillance than we were providing. We were busy with the many activities of three other children to give the proper time for personal attention, games, travel, homework, shopping, appointments, and, of course, love. (I think you get the big picture here. I feel like saying, "Trust me!")! To supply all of Matt's needs, especially extracurricular, was bringing our family into a state of mild frenzy. Not to mention the privacy of the neighborhood and Matt's safety. To live with this special need is to love and understand. Not living with this need, one is tempted to make judgments and have opinions.

The Benedictine School (Mary)

Matt entered the Benedictine School when he was fifteen, in the fall of 1985. Matt did extremely well at the school, located on the eastern shores of Maryland. Surrounded by farmland and a long beautiful tree-lined entrance, this school is favored by God, and destined to grow as it attends to the many diverse needs of its clients. The Open Community Homes have grown from two to seventeen!

We were blessed when Matt settled quickly into his new routine. Returning to school, after a weekend at home, he never seemed to be sad. Many of the children cried, at least, until their parents' cars were out of sight!

This is a wonderful school where hope, love, and respect always prevail. The able staff teaches these principles to each one, according to their needs.

As parents, Dick and I were confident that right choices had been made. Matt was exposed to classroom learning, and every single thing one needs to know about getting along in this great adventure called LIFE. Not to mention: Great fun! Not even once have we entertained a single regret about our decision to enter Matt into the Benedictine community. Truth be known, we could not afford to have him in a private school. Once again . . . GOD!

As we began to look for "just the right school," our visits

to many facilities left us saddened as we saw young people from whom little was expected. Their sad eyes showed no hope.

With a series of connections, a classmate, a newspaper article, and a phone call to a "Closed for the Summer" announcement on the answering machine, Sister Jeanette Murray, Director of the Benedictine School, returned our call. We all went to meet with the Sister for an interview, and the rest is history. We managed the issues of money because God made a way for us each month, each year, year-after-year! Looking back over those 25 years, we see clearly that GOD was in control!

(Matthew)

I entered the Benedictine School when I was fifteen. It is a wonderful school! I would go to school for three weeks, and then home on Friday with a bus ride to Wilmington. A long weekend with my family, and then a wonderful drive and lunch on our way back to the school was always enjoyed.

My first few years, I lived in a dorm with nine other boys. On the other side of the dorm were ten more boys. Sister was in the middle (in more ways than one!)!

I learned many things living with all these people. Two things I learned: Follow the rules, and, it is a good thing when a dime bounces off your bed!

(Mary)

During these early years at the Benedictine School, Matt began to voice his list of dreams. Number One on the list was to become a minister! the list was quite ambitious, including attending college, getting married, having a house, driving a car, and a few years later, owning a cell phone! To this day, Matt owns a cell phone! He has not achieved college, does not drive a car, and is not married. However, he is one of the greatest ministers I have met. To minister is to give. This is a service that flows from Matt with sincere love to everyone he meets. It is a gift from God!

!

Braces (Matthew)

When I was sixteen, my parents decided to get my teeth straightened. Dr. Toomey, a friend from Dewey Beach, was my orthodontist. His office was in Annapolis, Maryland, close to my school. He was the perfect choice for the job!

This was another time when God gave me just what I needed. The trip from my weekend home included my monthly visit to Dr. Toomey. The best part . . . lunch with mom and Mrs. Toomey. The braces did a great job, but I did not do MY job! The braces came off and I had to have gum surgery. It had been very hard for me to understand how to brush my teeth, so, Ouch!

(Mary)

On one of our rides to see Dr. Toomey, we got into the car and adjusted our seat belts, and I started the car. My custom was to put my coffee cup onto the well in front of the passenger seat.

More than a few times, on a quick stop or curve, the cup would topple-over. Matt was often the recipient of the contents from the cup. On this particular day, Matt looks at me, looks at the cup, and says, "Why not just pour it on me now and get it over with?"

Benedictine (Matthew)

When I went away to school, my sister Kim, and my brother, Michael, were still in high school. Pretty soon they were in college. A little later, David was working and living in an apartment. My brothers and sister were all married and out of my parent's house. Does that make me an ONLY CHILD? I never say how I missed them.

I loved school, being with friends, and all the loving teachers. We went to so many places like, The Naval Academy, Washington, D.C., New York, New York, to football games, plays, dinner theatres, Disney, Sight and Sound . . . and many more. Oh, I left out eating in restaurants, of course, my favorite!

Special Olympics was another one of my favorites in my hometown and at the Benedictine School. When I first attended Benedictine, I came home for the summer. The first summer I was home, I worked with Social Services in a sheltered workshop. My parents are proud of me when I always seem to say something positive about something I couldn't change anyway. I was fine and would choose another place to work next time!

Benedictine gave a play during Easter, and I played the part of Jesus. I hung on the cross, showing how He hung on the cross and died there for my sins. My parents came to see the play. I had a high fever, and so they took me home and straight to the hospital in Wilmington.

!

The Hospital Job (Matthew)

I was in the hospital a few days. Seems the nurses were so happy to meet me that they asked the Director of Personnel to come to my room to meet me. She was in charge of all the people who are hired at the hospital. I asked for a tour of the hospital. I happened to mention that I would love to work at their wonderful hospital. She signed me up for an all day training program to learn about the hospital and the things we needed to do for our jobs. I got the job!

When summer came, I started my job at the hospital. I was in the hospital kitchen, run by the Marriott. I scraped off dishes and put them in the dishwasher. Also, each day, I helped pack "Meals on Wheels," and helped fill trays for the patients.

One weekend, my boss gave me a ride on his motorcycle. Trust me, that was cool!

(Mary)

Matt was 16 when he worked at the hospital. We trusted him to ride his bike to work. He could discern the proper time to cross a very busy road and to come straight home. One day, following an interview with the hospital newsletter editor, Matt was so late that we became concerned. This was a special circumstance, and all was forgiven.

The Handicap That Wasn't (Mary)

All of these things I want to tell about Matthew Mason. He is a soul of pure joy, a sensitivity beyond belief, a most delightful sense of humor, to please is his desire. Joy! Joy! Joy!

Sandy-hair crew-cut, thick neck, short of stature, smiling with assurance that he can do anything. He is sensitive to almost any person's need. An example would be a pat on the shoulder, a smile, sometimes a question about one's feelings. Matt is a positive attitude in skin! By the time he was five, he had learned "politically correct" flattery and how to work a room like a "Pro." With confidence and poise, he uses his God-given talent to "feel out" the major; or shall we say, important people!

An attitude example: Someone might say, "Look at the trash on the lawn." Matt's answer would be: "Oh, do you want a job?" Every day is an adventure.

God had his hand on Matt from the very beginning. First the incubator cord, more than a few at home close calls, correcting the double-vision, healing his heart, and putting him in so many places where he learned and also ministered to so many different people. Many events seemed to involve a mike or a camera.

Newspapers were a large part of Matt's early life. There were many pictures and articles of encouragement for parents who were caring for their own Special Needs children. It seemed as if he drew people to himself. His gift of remembering names was overshadowed only by his incredible ability to spread joy and happiness to everyone in any situation.

Matt working a Fund Raiser at the Riverside Hospital "Fair"

The Life and Times of Matthew Mason
(Excerpted from the Hospital Newsletter)

Many of Riverside employees have had the pleasure of meeting Matthew Mason, one of our favorite food service employees. Matthew is a very eager young man with Down's syndrome who, through persistence and energy, found his own summer job. He was a patient at Riverside back in April and was so pleased with his care that he wanted to become an employee. And we were delighted to have him!

Approximately three years ago, Matthew, who is approaching his 22nd birthday, graduated from the Benedictine School for Exceptional Children. And Matthew is truly an exceptional person! He has many interests and talents. One of his key interests is sports! Although he enjoys many, his favorites are golf, wrestling and baseball. Matthew has even taken golf lessons and proudly professed that he is "very good!"

During his quiet time, Matthew enjoys sitting back and listening to music. He finds country music the most entertaining and relaxing and hopes one day to visit Nashville, the home of country music.

His interests does not stop there. Matthew also loves to travel. He travels with his family frequently and has visited places such as Connecticut, New York, and Disneyworld, and has enjoyed many trips to the beach.

Matthew also has an artistic side. According to his mother, he produces some wonderful hook rugs and would like to donate some of his best work to Riverside!

What really proves that Matthew is exceptional is that he is about to enter an independent living program. In September, he will share a house in Harmony Woods with two other men and will be working for Maryland Bank. the program is a learning experience and will teach them all of the responsibilities associated with work and home.

At the bank, Matthew is hoping to be involved with various office tasks such as sorting and delivering mail, copying, and tackling other duties as assigned. At home, Matthew will assume all the responsibilities of taking care of himself and the house. He will do the cooking, the cleaning, the laundry, etc.—and probably better than most! Matthew claims he is an expert at cooking spaghetti and meatballs.

Across the street from Matthew's new home is a house shared by three women who also are in the independent living program. These women currently work at Maryland Bank and have been extremely successful and happy. The two groups will participate in many shared activities and be each others support system.

His mother is fully confident that Matthew is ready for the program. He can do all these things now unsupervised and does a great job. Just last week, the Mason's were planning a dinner party. The day before the party, Matthew's parents had gone out to meet up with some friends and had left Matthew at home. Later that day, they came home to a wonderful surprise. Matthew had put together a beautifully decorated hors d'oeuvre tray, properly set the table with the fine china, crystal, and linen napkins, and vacuumed the entire downstairs—all in preparation for their guests!

At Riverside, Matthew assumes several roles in food service. He cleans the dishes, runs the dishwasher, puts things away, scrubs the pots and pans, and helps wrap the patient trays. He accepts each task with enthusiasm and an eagerness to help.

Riverside is grateful to employ Matthew. He is dedicated to his job and to Riverside. We will miss him when he begins his new position at the bank, but hope he will return to visit.

A fund-raiser with personality

Area celebrities will model for Holidazzle

By RHONDA B. GRAHAM
Staff reporter

WILMINGTON — Longwood Gardens is again the scene for the Holidazzle gala fashion show Friday.

The main conservatory opens at 6 p.m. with music and complimentary cocktails served in the Azalea Room. The fashion show runs from 7 to 8:30 in the Fern Room and ballroom. Models include personalities from the Greater Wilmington area, representing government, business, sports and television.

Leanne Evans, daughter of Mary Ann and Dave Evans, is this year's honorary "Holidazzle child." The 9-year-old Carrcroft Elementary School student has been a medal winner at the Delaware Special Olympics.

Co-chairs for the benefit this year are Katherine M. Klocko and Mathias J. Fallis. The benefit, in its 18th year, is the premiere fund-raiser for the Delaware Foundation for Retarded Children Inc. and regularly sells out. Table seating allows for a crowd of 800.

Eric Paul, a professional magician and juggler from Philadelphia, will perform.

"He has donated his services for the evening, along with the Phillie Phanatic and several other local magicians," Fallis said. "Rumor has it that if the governor is willing, he may be sawed in half as the show's grand finale."

Alicia Ahern, 26, and Matthew Mason, 22, former clients of the Benedictine School for Exceptional Children, are making a return appearance as guest models for the show.

Ahern, a clerical worker at MBNA, and Mason, a Riverside Hospital kitchen employee who soon will join the bank staff, modeled 10 years ago during the Delaware High School All-Star Football Game, another benefit that supports the DFRC.

Over the past 35 years, the DFRC has raised more than $3 million in seed money for vocational, educational and recreational programs, through the fashion show and football game.

Last year Holidazzle raised more than $79,000.

During 1990, the agency awarded $126,303 in grants to a number of supporting organizations, among them the Kent Sussex Industries sheltered workshop, the Delaware Parents of Downs Inc., the Stockley Center and Delaware Special Olympics.

The News Journal/JIM GRAHAM
Matthew Mason and Alicia Ahern will be making a return appearance as guest models for the Holidazzle fund-raiser on Friday.

Matt and Governor Henry DuPont

Mary Mason & Son Matt

Matt and His Father, Dick

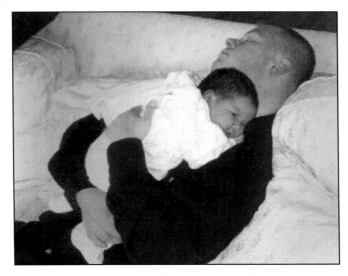

Matt and His Niece, Emily

The "Traveling" Man, Matt!

Matt as a Poster Child for United Way and DuPont
(Matt is in the Photo to the Left)

CHAPTER FOUR:

Adulthood

Age 36 (Mary)

There he is, dressed for the New Year's Eve celebration at the Country Club. Excitement filled the air at the Mason's house. Friends are all gathered and off we go to have a wonderful dinner and Matt's favorite activity—dancing!

Everyone is seated when I notice that Matt has a glass that looks as if it could contain champagne . . . surely not! My observation was correct, however. Matt calls the waitress over to tell her, "My champagne is quite sour!"

The evening proceeds . . . just before dinner is served, I notice that Matt is missing from the table . . . Dick finds him at the bar chatting with several young and pretty women, all enjoying a bourbon-on-the-rocks!

We do not encourage alcohol consumption, but a sip of wine and an occasional celebratory non-alcoholic beer on special occasions may be enjoyed.

I never cease to be amazed at the incredible sense of correct adult social behavior exhibited by Matt. We feel comfortable taking Matt into any environment and social situation. There is one exception—hugging. Sometimes it seems as if he loves so much that he just cannot squelch it. Matt has lost many a job because of his hugging.

True Friend (Mary)

More about the friend Matt had mentioned who was in prison. When Matt was allowed to speak to him, he would ask, "Are your eyes closed?" Then he would pray for him with all his heart. Never has his friend forgotten those simple, but oh, so sincere prayers.

!

Thoughts on Adulthood (Matthew)

Years go by and I am still so thankful for my life, my family, Mom, Dad, Michael, Kim, David, and my six nieces and nephews: James, Jeffrey, Kaine, Morgan, Emily and Julia. Julia said this one time: "I wish you could be me. I'm having a ball!" I feel the same way! I am thankful for God, His church, The Benedictine School and my friends.

My favorite things: Sports (especially golf), travel, reading, eating out, visiting my family, and I do like my jobs. Right now my jobs are at The Benedictine. I work in a commercial laundry, sometimes I.T.C. (Industrial Training Center). When spring comes, I will volunteer again with the Denton Country Club. I was there last fall and they really liked my work.

(Mary)

Matt has had opportunities for employment in the community through the years: a hospital, Marriott kitchen, NBNA Bank, college dining room, McDonald's, and many others.

!

The History of Golf, According to Matt

It all began when my parents moved to Hilton Head Island, South Carolina, in 1991. All three of us would attend The Heritage Golf Tournament at Harbour Town every spring, usually close to Easter, when I had my vacation.

My dad would buy a print, painted by Barry Horowitz (a famous artist who lives on Hilton Head). He painted The Harbour Town golf links. Guess what I did? I asked the golfers to sign my pictures! Greg Norman ("The Shark"), Davis Love, Payne Stewart, and former Vice President of the United States, Dan Quayle (He was teased about his spelling of potato).

I have signed gloves from Payne and Tom, and many signed golf balls and hats. Year-after-year I went with my parents to what is called the Heritage Pro AM Tournament. the pros golfed with men from the community. Those were the days I would get the signed balls and my pictures signed. My dad keeps these in a glass bowl in his office. We would also take pictures of the golfers.

The best things were the friendships made. Many times I have walked the course with Tom Lehman and his caddy, Andrew Martinez. One year Andrew let me carry Tom's BIG golf bag. Another time, Tom asked me to drive his ball from the 15th Tee. I always hit the ball straight! Trust Me! Well, I did hit the ball straight but only about 100 yards, then Tom started to put his tee down. His partners laughed and said, "Oh, no, your ball has already been hit!"

The very first golfer I met was Davis Love. He always gives me a golf ball and says, "Hello! How are you, Matt?"

In 1991, my Dad became a marshal on hole ten. After three years, he was changed to hole fourteen. This hole is pretty famous with the "pros." It is a par three and over water and really hard to make a good score. My mom and I would watch the tournament almost always at this hole. Sometimes I would watch alone while my mom worked at the tent for volunteers.

One day I asked my dad if I could go to the restroom (This was almost always a "tip off" to trouble on the way)! On my way back to hole fourteen, I saw Bob, a friend of our family. He asked if I needed anything, and I said I wanted to see my mom at the Volunteer tent. We took off in his golf cart and he got a call from someone and he had to leave me right in the middle of ??? I was lost, so I went to the first person I saw and told him my parent's name. My parents were looking everywhere for me until they saw, in big letters on the leader board, "WILL THE PARENTS OF MATTHEW MASON REPORT TO THE MAIN OFFICE!" I did hear a few words about that later!

!

Letter From Andrew Martinez, Cady for Tom Lehman

Jesus said, "The Kingdom of heaven belongs to such as these," in referring to the little children. My friend, Matt Mason, exemplifies the childlike, honest, open and endearingly loving attitude that I believe the Lord desires in all His children. I personally feel honored to spend time in Matt's presence. I never fail to get an attitude adjustment that is constantly needed.

I shall never forget the dinner party I attended with a few of my friends from the tour a few years ago. What began as an invitation turned into an evening prayer meeting lead by none other than Matt himself! I truly believe that the experience was a glimpse of what heaven will be like!

Letter From Ted Purdy, Pro Golfer

Sometimes in life you really need a hug. Matt Mason gave me a big one when I most needed it at the 2004 MCI Heritage on Hilton Head Island.

I was clinging to a one stroke lead at the biggest golf tournament of my life. This was my big chance on the PGA Tour. A win would make my career and ensure that I would never have to return to the hardscrabble life on Asian Tour, where I had toiled in previous years. Not to mention, the $900,000 first place prize money would certainly be a life-changing payday!

The first three days of the tournament, I had played great and built a comfortable lead. On the final day, the title had come down to a fight between myself and seasoned pro, Stewart Cink, who had played well in the morning and was the clubhouse leader.

With no one else contending, the CBS Sports cameras followed me all day. Pressure sure mounts when you're constantly under the blisteringly critical microscopes of the likes of announcers Gary McCord and David Feherty. Heck, they were even commenting about how much gum I was chewing and wondering what my breath smelled like after eating the raw broccoli that I had brought along for an energy snack!

I may have felt some jitters. Golf became a little more difficult. I had frequent birdie looks the first three days, but this day I was having to scrape pars together.

On the fourteenth hole, I sailed my tee shot long and left over the green, an indication of nerves. I had to hit one of the best chip shots of my life and then make a slippery 10-foot putt to save par there. The crowd erupted when my putt curled in. I was pumped!

Matt Mason, who was working as a marshal at the 14th green, gave me a big "thumbs up!" I smiled back and tossed him the golf ball. He grabbed it, clutched it for a moment and then sprang forward to give me a big bear-hug of thanks. It was awesome!

I think Matt's hug emboldened me for the rest of the tournament, which Cink won on the fifth playoff hole. It was a heck of a match.

I think I won more that day with Matt's genuine gesture

of happiness and appreciation than if I had pulled out the victory. Matt's hug taught me to always look around and appreciate and thank the people around me. Now, I always make it a point to thank the volunteers at golf tournaments. It's a small and simple thing to say thank you, but as Matt's awesome reaction taught me, those small, simple acts of gratitude will stay in people's hearts forever!

The video of what my brother calls his favorite moment in sports still lives on YouTube. Whenever I need inspiration or perspective, I'll call up that video and listen to CBS announcer Jim Nantz's voice almost crack during that moment of pure joy. Warms my heart every time! Thank you, Matt!

The next year during the Pro Am play, here comes Ted, walking toward the putting green on Hole 14. He called to Matt to come and putt his ball into the hole. I'm sure I saw Dick's knuckles go white!

With all the confidence of a professional, Matt steps up and taps the ball. Rolling, rolling, two feet, three feet and four feet to a victorious entrance into the cup at HOLE FOURTEEN! This was huge to anyone who knows Hole 14, and how very difficult this hole is to putt. The clapping was great and Dick's knuckles returned to normal!

The Presbyterian Men's Heritage Breakfast in Hilton Head (Matthew)

In 1997, I was asked to pray at the Presbyterian Men's Heritage Breakfast in Hilton Head. Almost 800 people were there, and Mr. John Scott asked ME to pray!

The speaker was Tom Lehman. He was so kind to me. The beginning of my friendship with him and his caddy, Andrew Martinez, began on that day. Each year, during The Heritage, we get together with Andrew. Sometimes he brings his caddy friends to have a dinner with us. I look forward to these times because we all share Jesus and His love. I really love the way they love me! Once, when my parents lived in Sea Pines, they invited Steve, "Doc", Andrew and a few others. We had pizza and stuff and a group prayer time. My mom called the prayer the best food!

Five years ago, in 2004, the tournament asked me to be a marshal on hole fourteen with my dad! I have been a marshal now of that hole for five years, and it's almost time for The Heritage again.

In 2004, when Ted Purdy walked from hole 14 towards me, I gave a big "thumbs up" to him. He tossed me his play ball and, Oh, yes, I hugged him! (I think he hugged me too!) Now my dad and anyone who had anything to do with The Heritage were VERY upset!

(Mary)

As co-captain on hole 14, Dick Mason was mentally see-ing his and Matthew's days of volunteering gone forever! CBS and local media picked up the "Incident" and this left Matthew in a rather wonderful new frame or fame!

The glorious end to this story is that Ted Purdy donated $50,000 to The Benedictine School. The next year, during the Pro AM play, here comes Ted walking towards the putting green on hole 14. He called to Matt to come and putt his ball into the hole. I am sure I saw Dick's knuckles go white!

With all the confidence of a professional, Matt steps up and taps the ball. Rolling, rolling, two feet, three feet, and four feet, to a victorious entrance into the cup at HOLE FOURTEEN!

This was huge to anyone who knew hole fourteen and how difficult this hole is to putt. The clapping was great, and Dick's knuckles returned to normal shortly thereafter.

Over the years, there are so many stories about Matt and his special friends. It seems as if half the fans who pass through the proudly held ropes at hole fourteen, greet Matt by name with encouraging comments. Matt's job is to hold the ropes, keeping the crowds back, until the golfers, caddies and other officials have passed on to the next hole. This past April (2009), Matt received his five year pin.

The ambassador of hole 14

BY CHRISTOPHER WUENSCH
ISLAND TODAY

Boo Weekley may own the Verizon Heritage, but hole No. 14 belongs to Matt Mason.

The Heritage Foundation recognized Mason and other volunteers this week with commemorative pins, denoting the number of years they've dedicated to Sea Pines' annual PGA Tour stop.

For the 38-year-old Mason, a Hilton Head resident with Down syndrome, this year's tourney marked his fifth at his favorite perch on the 14th green.

His official job is to raise the "Quiet" placard before putts and to seal off the ropes to the public when the golfers are done. Unofficially, however, Mason's job is a goodwill ambassador and head cheerleader for the golfers that pass through.

"That's my hole," he beamed between hugs after the day's final pairings — including Weekley en route to winning his second-consecutive Heritage — passed through.

A mentally locked-in Weekley didn't return Mason's outstretched hand for a high-five, but the TidePointe resident did score one from Anthony Kim, Weekley's pairing partner for the afternoon and tourney runner-up.

Interactions with golfers are commonplace for Mason, who wears a straw-fedora with an autograph by Brandt Snedeker on the crown.

Four years ago, Mason responded to a gift of a golf ball from the PGA's Ted Purdy on 14 by throttling the 2004 Heritage runner-up with an affectionate bear hug. Purdy, who witnesses say just "fell

Matt Mason has volunteered on the 14th hole at the Verizon Heritage golf tournament for the past five years.

into the hug," responded by donating $50,000 to Mason's Benedictine School in Ridgely, Md.

"He's always trying to help," said Mason's father Richard Mason, who also volunteers at the Heritage.

The Heritage Foundation recognized many other volunteers for their tireless efforts during the tournament, including Marian McDuffie, who has worked all 40 Verizon Heritages.

God willing, both McDuffie and Mason will be back next year for another go-around with the Heritage. Mason will be easy to find. He'll be the one standing guard on No. 14 — his hole.

For the record, after being interviewed, Matt Mason planted one of his famous bear hugs on BT Sports Editor **Christopher Wuensch**. It was the highlight of Wuensch's week at the Heritage. Contact Wuensch at 815-0814 or by e-mail at sports@blufftontoday.com.

A Very Special Hug

Thanks to Matt, a resident in one of our group homes, Benedictine has received a $50,000 contribution from the MCI Heritage Classic Foundation. For years, Matt has worked alongside his father, a volunteer marshal at the 14th hole of the MCI Heritage Golf Tournament. This year, as the professionals came off the 14th green, Matt would give them a big smile, a high five and in some cases a hug. On the last day, Ted Purdy received his hug, captured on national TV. Mr. Purdy went on to place second in the Tournament and designated Benedictine as the recipient of $50,000 from the Heritage Classic Foundation.

MCI Heritage

Pro Golfer, Tom Lehman, with Matthew being Interviewed

Tom Lehman's caddy, Andrew Martinez

Matt's Prayer for the
Christian Heritage Breakfast
at the Crowne Plaza Resort
April 15, 1997

This event was sponsored by
The Presbyterian Men of the Church
Hilton Head Island, South Carolina

Davis Love III, Matt & Mark

CHAPTER FIVE:

Life Today (Mary)

At this writing, Matthew resides in Denton, Maryland, in a residence called "The Benedictine Foundation Open Community Home." Proudly, we can say, they operate 17 homes in Maryland and four in Delaware!

Matt and three other young men live, work, and play not so differently from most. These young men are lovingly assisted by "live in" counselors, a blessing we can barely comprehend!

!

ABOUT THE AUTHOR
Mary Mason

I am grateful to God! He gives me strength, encouragement, joy, and sometimes a clear mind. It is such a time as this that I write of our fourth child, Matthew. My husband, Dick, and I have been blessed to be Matthew's parents, knowing that God chose us to be so honored.

This book is offered for hope to all. An adventure of love, joy, peace, and a growing understanding of God, Jesus Christ, and The Holy Spirit. Thirty-nine years I have collected pictures, news articles, stories, memories and quotes. My original title for this telling was "Trust Me!", Matt's favorite quip. After an article appeared in Hilton Head Today in 2008, I fell in love with the name Chris Wuench gave to Matt. Thanks Chris! THE AMBASSADOR OF THE FOURTEENTH HOLE was given birth. A story of how God has us under His Wings, never leaving us, always loving us, and using us for His glory.

There are many stories yet to be told of how Matt exudes his Christian love to all he meets. It seems that sometimes he has a love affair with all the world!

Praying that you will find joy and maybe a few tears from this story framed by God, told by one unable to tell it, except through God's amazing grace. Thank You, Father.

Mary Mason
January 2010

!

A Few of Matt's Accomplishments

Fund raiser, newspaper carrier, Boy Scouts, Gold-Silver-Blue and Red medals and Ribbons Winner from Special Olympics, Golfer, traveler, swimmer, fisherman, biker, plays guitar-drums-and piano, dancer, horse groomer, maker of cotton candy and Latch Hook Rugs, bowler, tennis player, skier, ski boat driver, gardener, preacher, scribe, uses computers, plans menus and schedules of any kind!

A Few Words From Some Friends
of The Family

(From Joyce Toomey—Dewey Beach)
Matt's Orthodontist's Wife

I met Matt when he was five. He knew everyone on the
block and the location of the nearest donut shop! Our children grew up together. Matthew was always part of the gang.
He knew when someone needed a hug. He still does.

Knowing Matt and his family is a treasure that is held in
your heart. A small special child has grown into a lovely man
with a fine sense of humor and a deep faith in God. He's
more than special—He's the Best!

(From Jim & Bernice Tatum)

We are in the sunset years of our lives and many wonderful people have crossed our paths. We will tell you about
one of them.

A joyful, delightful and enthusiastic young man walked
into our hearts and lives one Sunday morning when Dick and
Mary Mason introduced their son, Matthew, to us and to the
Adult Sunday School Class.

Matt was always eager to speak and the class was delighted to see and hear him. One Sunday—without checking

with his mother—he invited ALL 100 OF US to come to his house the next week to celebrate his birthday!

He shared with us how much he loves the Lord and the Lord's people. When he came to the end, he would lead us in prayer which warmed our hearts and thrilled our spirits. We could sense a real, personal relationship and walk with God. He was made an honorary member of the Jim Tatum Class.

Matt was friendly to all. His greeting to Bernice was always, "Hello, Beautiful!" To Jim, he often said, "I love you more than the others!"

Malachi 3 teaches that God will remember those who love, fear, honor and respect Him. Verse 17 says, "They shall be mine . . . in that day when I make up my jewels" (King James Version of the Holy Bible). We believe that Matt will be one of the brightest jewels of them all!

!

Life Today For Matthew

SMILE FOR THE CAMERA

JON M. FLETCHER/The Times-Union
Jaguars fan Matthew Mason (right) points Jaguars offensive tackle Samuel Gutekunst (60) toward a relative with a camera following practice Monday morning on the practice field outside Jacksonville Municipal Stadium.

Matthew's 2009 Housemates

Matthew—the Competitor!

Epilogue (Dick Mason)

This story has been about our son, Matthew Jarrett Mason, and was written by his mother, Mary Mason. It has described Matt's very scary start in life when doctors were very pessimistic with their projections. It has described the challenges that mother and son overcame during his first several years. As Matt grew, he developed a cheerful attitude, a loving, caring nature, and enjoyed family and friends to the fullest.

At age 40, Matt continues to love a party, is a crowd pleaser, pleasant, and is a God-loving young man with social graces and personality, giving him the ability to socialize with the boss or the laborer.

To give credit where due, his mother provided the foundation in Matt's early years and her responses to challenges were rewarded. Matt was included in all of her daily activities that developed his interests in bible studies, social meetings and group gatherings. By the age of six, Matt's story mirrors that of "Rudolf-the-Red-Nosed-Reindeer," as he developed skills to be the leader and the guy that good things could happen to.

At age 14, Matt was accepted by the Benedictine School for Exceptional Children in Ridgely, Maryland. Sister Jeanette and her staff became the dominate adults molding Matt's character and training him to live a normal life. The

Benedictine Foundation has provided love, caring, guidance and joy for Matt.

We are very proud of our son and his accomplishments, as well as his opportunist attitude. Matt is the happiest young man I know!

Thank you for reading this accounting of Matt's life. I do hope that you have enjoyed the message. Perhaps you will share this book with others, whom you may know, who might find encouragement by reading "The Ambassador of the 14th Hole."

Obviously, we are very pleased with The Benedictine School and would encourage anyone interested to contact them at **1-410-634-1990** or write to them with an inquiry or a contribution at:

**The Benedictine Foundation
14299 Benedictine Lane
Ridgely, Maryland 21660**

!

In His Steps Publishing Company
6500 Clito Road
Statesboro, Georgia 30461
(912) 587-4400